Grab - and let g

GW01048670

Written by Clare Beswick and Sally Featherstone
Illustrated by Martha Hardy

A *Little Baby Book*™
Published by Featherstone Education

Featherstone Education

Key to stages of development

Heads up lookers and communicators

Sitters, standers and explorers

Movers, shakers and players

Walkers, talkers and pretenders

About Little Baby Books

Grab - and let go is one in a series of Little Baby Books, intended to help you to implement **'Birth to Three Matters,** *a framework to support children in their earliest years'* (DfES/Sure Start 2002). Each Little Baby Book focuses on a small range of components from one of the aspects of the Framework, and contains a range of activities suitable for you to use with the babies and children in your care.

Every activity is explained, with details of:
* a suggested stage of development
* the resources and equipment you will need
* how to organise the activity
* ways of extending the core activity
* how to adapt the activity for children with additional needs
* what you might observe and note as the activity progresses
* how you and the parents/carers can work together to reinforce and enhance children's learning
* details of what the babies and children are learning through the activity.

At the bottom corner of each page, you will see two of our cover children, who represent the stage of development where the activity might be particularly useful, although of course, you can use the activities with children at other ages and stages. The key (in the left hand margin of this page) follows the Framework areas of development:
* Heads up, lookers and communicators (0 to 8 months)
* Sitters, standers and explorers (8 to 18 months)
* Movers, shakers and players (18 to 24 months)
* Walkers, talkers and pretenders (24 to 36 months).

2

About 'Grab - and let go'

The development of fine motor skills in under threes is an exciting process, opening up the world of exploration and independence for babies and young children. It contributes to their discovery of the effect they can have on their world and on the people who are most important to them. It is a staged process with most babies and young children developing and refining their fine motor skills stage by stage. The age at which they reach each stage is hugely variable, but much can be done to provide opportunities for children to practise and progress their skills as they reach each of the stages.

The activities in this book will enable parents and practitioners working with under threes to provide interesting enjoyable play at each stage in a baby and young child's development of fine motor skills. The activities encourage:

* reaching and patting
* grabbing and holding
* releasing
* giving and taking objects
* two hands together
* isolating index fingers

* using separate fingers
* finger and thumb pincer
* clapping hands
* using tools and mark making
* handling small objects
* hand eye co-ordination
* rolling and throwing.

On each activity page there are plenty of ideas to practise each skill and advice on how to take it on to the next stage. Look out for our tiny tips and suggestions on how to adapt the activities for children with individual or special needs.

Aspect:
A Healthy Child
Components:
Growing and developing

Why are these activities so important?

Babies and children need to touch and experience things first hand. Contact with real things and people builds links between brain cells and this helps learning. There is also evidence that babies and children will develop more quickly if they have a good mix of playing with real things (hairbrushes, pans, spoons, adult shoes and clothes for example), and purpose made toys. This is why many of the activities in this book use real, everyday things.

Playing with real things enables babies:

    to explore the things they see around them, feeling textures and surfaces
    to focus on objects and people and begin to recognise familiar features
    to use both hands, and bring things towards the mid line of their bodies
    to learn to pass things from hand to hand, to hold and release, give and take
    to squeeze, poke, stroke, pull, pat, developing the muscles in fingers and hands.

Playing with real things helps older children:

    to put things under, in, through, on, behind, developing a sense of position
    to develop their hand/eye co-ordination
    to learn the names and features of objects
    to hold, roll, catch, throw, place objects with increasing accuracy
    to describe textures and surfaces
    to compare, contrast, create
    to imitate, pretend and imagine.

And of course, babies and children develop more quickly if they have the support and company of gentle, loving adults who know them well and get involved in their play. The encouragement, language, example and inspiration of the caring adult is vital to children's growth. They need you with them, helping them make sense of the world.

Watch, listen, reflect

Assessing babies' and children's learning is a difficult process, but we do know that any assessment must be based on careful observation of children in action.

On each activity page, you will see a box labelled **Watch, listen, reflect.** This box contains suggestions of what you might look and listen for as you work and play with the babies and children. Much of the time you will watch, listen and remember, using your knowledge of early years and of the children and reflecting on the progress of the individual child. These informal observations will help you to plan the next day's or week's activities.

However, sometimes, what you see is new evidence - something you have never seen the child do before, or something which concerns you. In these cases you might make a written note of the achievements you see, or the concern you have, noting the date and time you observed it. You will use these notes for a range different purposes, some of which are:

- 👁 to remind you of the event or achievement (it's easy to forget in a busy setting!)
- 👁 to use in discussion with your manager or other practitioners
- 👁 to contribute to the child's profile or record
- 👁 to discuss with parents
- 👁 to help with identifying or supporting additional needs
- 👁 to help with planning for individuals
- 👁 to make sure you tell everyone about the child's achievements.

Observation is a crucial part of the complex job you do, and time spent observing and listening to children is never wasted.

Aspect:
A Healthy Child
Components:
Growing and developing

Keeping safe

Safety must be the top priority when working with any baby or young child, in a nursery or at home. All the activities in Little Baby Books are safe for under threes, given suitable supervision. You will already have a health and safety policy but here are just a few tips for safe playing with babies and young children.

Watch for choking hazards

Young babies and children naturally explore toys by bringing them to their mouths. This is fine, but always check that toys are clean. If you think there might be a risk of choking, check with a choke measure. You can get one from a high street baby shop.

Never leave babies or young children unattended

Babies and young children are naturally inquisitive and this needs to be encouraged, BUT they need you to watch out for them. Make sure you are always there.

Check for sharp edges

Some everyday objects or wooden toys can splinter. Check all toys and equipment regularly. Don't leave this to chance – make a rota.

Ribbons and string

Mobiles and toys tied to baby gyms are a great way to encourage looking and reaching, – but do check regularly that they are fastened securely. Ribbons and string are fascinating for babies and children of all ages, but they can be a choking hazard.

Clean spaces

Babies are natural explorers. They need clean floors. Store outdoor shoes away from the under threes area.

Sitters and standers

Make sure of a soft landing for babies and young children who are just beginning to manage sitting and standing balance. Put a pillow behind babies who are starting to sit. Keep the area clear of hard objects, such as wooden bricks. Look out for trip hazards for crawlers and walkers.

High and low chairs

Make sure babies and young children are fastened securely into high chairs and that chairs are moved out of the way when not in use. Use a low chair and table for young children. Try making a foot-rest if their feet don't reach the ground. Avoid chairs that tip easily.

Contents

Aspect:
A Healthy Child

Components:
Growing and developing

Heads up lookers and communicators

Aspect:
A Healthy Child

Components:
Growing and developing

Reach it -
black and white patterns

What you need

* white card
* black card or paper
* scissors, glue and ribbon
* hoop or baby gym

What you do

1. Cut different shapes, such as zigzags from the black card, and glue to the white card to make black and white contrasting patterns. Make different patterns on each side of the white card.
2. Tie the cards securely to the hoop or baby gym. Lay the baby under the baby gym or suspend the hoop securely so that the cards are within easy reach.
3. Tap the cards and encourage the baby to look at and reach to pat the cards.

another idea:
* Try tiny black and white spots or chequer board patterns.

Ready for more?

✋ Cut eyes, noses and mouths to make black and white face patterns.
✋ Add a reflective border to the cards. Help the baby hold the card with two hands.

Individual needs

☼ Some babies will need you to take their hand gently to the cards.

☼ Tape bells to the back of the card. Shake to help the baby focus and look in the direction of the sound.

☼ Try sitting the baby in a baby relaxer under the hoop or baby gym.

Tiny Tip

✳ Young babies focus best on faces and objects held at about 22cm (9 inches).

Watch, listen, reflect

👁 See which patterns are most appealing to the baby.

👁 Watch where the baby can most easily see and reach for the cards.

👁 Listen and copy any sounds they make.

Working together

Parents could:

* tell practitioners which are their baby's favourite pictures or mobiles.
* try out the cards at home.

Practitioners could:

* show parents the cards and how they are being used.
* visit the library to borrow black and white pattern baby books, and look out for black and white pattern soft toys.

Grab - and let go

Developing fine motor skills

What are they learning?

are they
   looking?
   turning to sound?
   reaching?
   sharing fun?
this leads to
   * grabbing
   * holding

9

Heads up lookers and communicators

Aspect:
A Healthy Child

Components:
Growing and developing

Pat it! -
texture and treasure

What you need

* a shallow plastic tray
* different textured objects - crinkly paper, a woolly sock, furry glove, toothbrush, hard plastic cup, etc

What you do

Sit on the floor opposite the baby.
1. Make a treasure tray. Place the different textured objects on the tray. Tap the objects on the tray.
2. Talk and sing to the baby as you play. Help them to explore the objects.
3. Try rubbing the different textures firmly but gently on the backs of their hands.
4. Encourage them to reach for and pat the objects with two hands.
5. Praise the baby's efforts at reaching with words, cuddles, gentle strokes and tickles.

another idea:
* Try patting warm, damp, bubbly sponges.

Ready for more?

- Put together a tray of different textured wooden objects to pat.

- Offer the objects one at a time for the baby to grasp and hold.

Individual needs

✿ Make sure the baby is sat securely. It is hard to reach and pat objects if you are still working on your sitting balance!

✿ Lift each object, show it to the child, press it gently into their hands and then tap the tray as you return it for them to reach for.

Tiny Tip

❋ Stuff a small cushion or rolled up tea towel next to the baby if their highchair is too wide.

Watch, listen, reflect

👁 Watch for any textures that the baby really likes or dislikes.

👁 Look to see if they are content to pat the objects or are trying to grab the objects.

👁 Listen to the range of sounds they are making.

Working together

Parents could:

* bring objects from home for their baby's treasure tray.
* tell the practitioner which objects their baby likes to reach for or pat.

Practitioners could:

* share with parents the different objects their baby has enjoyed on the treasure tray.
* play together for a few moments, talking with parents about imitating the sounds the baby makes in play.

Grab - and let go

Developing fine motor skills

What are they learning?

are they
   feeling textures?
   sitting & patting?
   looking/reaching?
   showing pleasure?
   exploring?
this leads to
   * grasping & holding
   * shaking
   * letting go

11

Developing fine motor skills

Heads up lookers and communicators

Aspect:
A Healthy Child

Components:
Growing and developing

12

Grab it -
sticks and shakers

What you need
* rattles
* home made or bought shakers
* small wooden spoons
* ribbons

What you do

1. Sit opposite the baby and hold the rattle out for them to reach for. Hold it in the mid line.
2. Shake it, call the baby's name and gently lift their arm from the elbow towards the rattle or shaker. Help them to grasp the rattle, shake it and share their enjoyment of the sound.
3. Tie the ribbons together in a bundle. Trail them through the baby's outstretched hands. Encourage them to grasp the ribbons, or gently twine the ribbons over both hands.
4. Offer the wooden spoon to the baby to grab and hold. Hold the spoon with them and sing 'Shake, shake, shake, tap, tap, tap'.

another idea:
* Chiffon scarves are great for reaching and grabbing.

Ready for more?

- Hold the shakers to either side for the baby to practise reaching to the side.
- Provide a plastic bowl full of ribbons or scarves to reach for, grab and explore.

Individual needs

☼ Some babies and children need lots of encouragement to reach and grab. Try reflective objects, such as a baby mirror. Tie bells to the mirror for further encouragement.

☼ Make sure the baby or child is sitting well supported if necessary.

Tiny Tip

✳ During everyday care, give the baby suitable objects to feel before using them, such as feeling their vest before putting it on, or holding the flannel before washing.

Watch, listen, reflect

👁 Watch which hand the baby finds easiest to reach and grab with.

👁 Watch to see if they are bringing the shaker to their mouth to explore.

👁 Watch and listen to how they express their feelings, maybe excitement, pleasure, or perhaps dislike of each object.

Working together

Parents could:

* bring in some everyday objects from home for their baby to reach for, such as a soft hairbrush, flannel, plastic spoon and so on.
* offer their baby objects from both sides.

Practitioners could:

* look out for interesting objects to encourage reaching.
* make practising reaching a part of everyday activities, such as meal times and changing times.

Grab - and let go

Developing fine motor skills

What are they learning?

are they
　reaching?
　grasping?
　exploring?
　making sounds?
　having an effect?
this leads to
　* cause & effect
　* fine motor
　　control

13

Aspect:
A Healthy Child

Components:
Growing and developing

Let Go! -
grab and let go splashes

What you need

* small sponges
* flannel
* warm water
* tin lid or plastic tray

What you do

1. Soak the sponges and flannel in warm water.
2. Sit opposite the baby and offer the sponges and flannels one at a time.
3. Encourage them to grab the sponge, squeeze and then drop onto the tray.
4. Play alongside the baby, squeezing and dropping the sponge onto the tin lid.
5. Share the fun with smiles and say 'Drip, drip', and then when the sponge has been dropped, say and gesture 'Gone'.

another idea:

* Add some 'no tears' shampoo bubbles to the warm water and encourage babies to grab and pop bubbles.

Ready for more?

* Put the sponges and flannel in an empty ice cream box. Help the baby to lift them from the carton, squeeze and then release.
* Try the same with warm cooked spaghetti or pasta ribbons.

14

Individual needs

☼ Some babies and children dislike certain textures. Vary the feel of the items to meet individual needs.

☼ Gently squeeze the warm water on to the back of their hand if the baby is reluctant to reach for the sponges.

☼ Give them plenty of time to explore.

Tiny Tip

❋ Stroking gently on the back of the baby's hand will help them to let go of objects.

Watch, listen, reflect

👁 Look carefully at how the baby grips the flannel. Are they using their whole hand, or starting to use fingers and thumbs together?

👁 Watch and listen to how the baby asks for 'More'. How do they respond to the word and gesture 'Gone'?

Working together

Parents could:

* try this activity at home at bath time, and tell practitioners how they have got on.
* share some finger and tickle rhymes with their baby.

Practitioners could:

* share their observations with parents.
* make time every day for some finger rhyme fun, and show them to parents.

What are they learning?

are they
  releasing?
  exploring?
  looking?
  asking for more?
  sharing fun?
this leads to
  * fine motor control
  * sharing
  * first words

Look at Me - mirror play

What you need

* safety mirror
* hat
* shiny plastic bangle

What you do

1. Sit next to the baby so you can both see your reflections.
2. Sing 'Hello' to the baby, smiling and reaching for the mirror. Encourage the baby to reach for reflections in the mirror.
3. Put the hat on your head and then tip it off slowly, saying 'Gone'. Offer them the hat to put back on your head. Tip it off gently with smiles and 'Gone'.
4. Encourage them to reach for and lift the hat themselves, putting it back on your or their own head.
6. Praise their reaching and lifting, with smiles and then the 'Tipping it off again' game.

another idea:
* Use a small play mirror that the baby can hold. Sing 'Hello' to the baby, looking together at your reflections in the mirror.

Ready for more?

- Dab some yoghurt on your nose and encourage the baby to reach and explore your face.
- Use a 'no tears' shampoo to make some froth on a play mirror. Rub away the bubbles to see the reflection.

Individual needs

☼ Be sure to hold the mirror very close for babies and children with visual difficulties.

☼ Play the tipping the hat off game face to face with babies, before trying it with the mirror.

☼ Make sure any child with poor head control or balance is well supported.

Tiny Tip

✼ Take extra care with bubble play with young babies. The mixture may really sting their eyes.

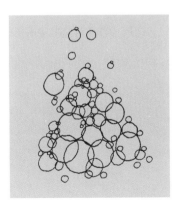

Watch, listen, reflect

◉ Watch to see how the baby shows excitement and anticipation of the hat falling.

◉ Think about all the different ways they are communicating without words, such as facial expression, looking, pointing.

◉ Watch how reaching affects their sitting balance. Are they using one hand to support themselves?

Working together

Parents could:

* sing hello to their baby in the mirror each morning.
* play Peek-a-boo in the mirror.

Practitioners could:

* make mirror play a part of the baby's changing routine.
* place mirrors low enough for babies and young children to see their own reflections as they play.

Grab - and let go

Developing fine motor skills

What are they learning?

are they
   looking?
   reaching?
   grasping?
   sharing attention?
   exploring faces?
this leads to
  * fine motor control
  * understanding

Sitters, standers and explorers

Aspect:
A Healthy Child

Components:
Growing and developing

Two Hands Together -
squeezing and pulling

What you need

* net fabric
* dry sponge
* small, soft ball
* hair scrunchies

What you do

For babies with good sitting balance spread the items around the floor within easy reach.

1. Encourage them to reach for, grasp and hold each item. Play together at squeezing and pulling each item. Encourage them to use two hands together.
2. Sit younger babies in a high chair and encourage them to grab the items from the tray, pulling and scrunching together.
3. Try lying babies on the floor and placing one item on their tummy. Prompt them with words and tickles to reach for and grasp with two hands, bringing the item up so that they can look and feel.

another idea:
* Put the objects in a small bag for squeezing and pulling out.

Ready for more?

Stuff a small soft ball in a sock. Try pulling the ball out of the sock. Put a sock loosely on your hands. Play together helping the baby to pull the sock off your hands.

Individual needs

☼ Some babies and children find using two hands together difficult. Make sure they are sitting supported, so they can focus on their reaching, without risking toppling over.

☼ Use just one noisy toy, such as a soft toy that squeaks when you squeeze it.

Tiny Tip

✳ Ask parents to bring scrunchies and other squeezing items.

Watch, listen, reflect

👁 Check out which toys, sounds and textures are most appealing to each baby.

👁 Look at the way they are exploring the toys, such as shaking, squeezing or banging.

👁 Listen to the sounds they make. What feelings are they expressing?

Working together

Parents could:

* put their baby's favourite comfort toy on their baby's tummy for them to reach for and grasp.
* tell practitioners how their baby explores favourite toys.

Practitioners could:

* make sure babies have plenty of uninterrupted time to explore the toys.
* make a collection of toys for pulling and scrunching together and keep it easily to hand.

Grab - and let go

Developing fine motor skills

What are they learning?

are they
 using 2 hands?
 exploring cause
 & effect?
 sharing fun?
 attending?
this leads to
 * exploring play
 * understanding
 object use

19

In and Out -
filling and tipping play

What you need

* everyday objects such as a sock, spoon, flannel, bowl, teddy, plastic keys, baby board book
* an empty ice cream tub or similar container

What you do

1. Sit opposite the baby and offer them the objects one at a time to explore.
2. Show them how the objects are used, eg wipe the flannel on your face and then gently on their face, and say 'Look, wash faces'.
3. Give them plenty of time to explore each object and then drop it into the ice cream tub. Stroke the back of their hand gently to help them let go. Say 'Gone' as the object drops into the tub.

another idea:
* Play dropping soft toys into a large cardboard box, and then tipping them out again!

Ready for more?

- Try small objects and a shoebox with lid.
- Stuff teddy bears or old clothes into a pillowcase, and then pull them out again.
- Play at posting small balls into a hole in a cardboard box.

Individual needs

☼ Use noisy sound-making toys for filling and tipping play with children who need more encouragement and support.
☼ Use bright shiny or fluorescent coloured toys for babies and children needing help with looking and grasping.
☼ Use light objects such as scarves for children with physical difficulties.

Tiny Tip

❋ Put a list of items you need on the parents' notice board – such as pillowcases, shoe boxes and so on.

Watch, listen, reflect

◉ Observe how pleasure or satisfaction is shown.
◉ Look out for the baby or young child imitating your actions and gestures.
◉ Listen for sounds and first words.
◉ Praise reaching and grasping.

Working together

Parents could:

* play at tipping and filling boxes together at home.
* save washed ice cream cartons and shoeboxes.

Practitioners could:

* explain the importance of the activity to parents. It can be very irritating if you don't understand the value of this sort of play!
* make sure collections of everyday objects are together, clean and easily to hand.

Grab – and let go

Developing fine motor skills

What are they learning?

are they
   using objects?
   understanding first words?
   grasping?
   releasing?
   filling/emptying?
this leads to
  * understanding object words
  * copying

Movers, shakers and players

Aspect:
A Healthy Child

Components:
Growing and developing

First Fingers -
index finger fun

What you need

* small plastic cups and plates
* cooked noodles
* jelly
* yoghurt
* bread

What you do

1. Spread a tiny drop of runny yoghurt on to a plastic plate or tray. Stuff bits of bread and pasta in the cups.
2. Put a tiny drop of runny yoghurt on the baby's and your own index fingers. Trail your index fingers around the plate, making patterns and swirls. Stop and place your index fingers on the child's index fingers. Play at tapping the sticky fingers together. Add more yoghurt to index fingers and enjoy sliding fingers back and forth and round and round in the goo.
3. Play at poking and prodding index fingers into the plastic cups. Take turns with the child to prod and poke. Feel the different shapes and textures.

another idea:
* Try poking holes in pizza, jelly or bread dough.

Ready for more?

- Play 'Round and round the garden', taking turns to use the first finger to show teddy going round and round the garden.
- Use a toy keyboard. Encourage each child to play first with index fingers and then to use each finger separately.

22

Individual needs

☼ Remember that some children may be really sensitive on their hands and intensely dislike some textures and consistencies.

☼ Some children may need lots of very simple individual finger play, such as tapping fingers, pointing and prodding, to help them isolate their index finger.

Tiny Tip

❋ Check out the Little Book of Nursery Rhymes and This Little Puffin for a comprehensive collection of traditional finger rhymes.

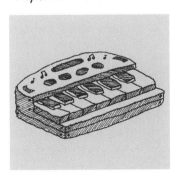

Watch, listen, reflect

👁 Watch out for emerging hand preference. Look carefully at the way children pick up objects, how they use their fingers and thumbs.

👁 Observe how children use a pointing gesture to support their first words.

👁 Listen to and encourage children to combine words, pointing and gesture.

Working together

Parents could:

* tell practitioners their child's favourite rhymes.
* allow for messy food play and finger feeding at mealtimes.
* find out why finger play is so important.

Practitioners could:

* get together with colleagues and make a list of all the finger rhymes they know, and share these with parents and the children regularly.
* make time every day to share a finger rhyme individually with their key children.

What are they learning?

are they
  isolating index fingers?
  using fingers & thumbs together?
  exploring?
  trying new things?
  making sounds?
this leads to
  * pincer grip
  * pencil control

Grab - and let go

Developing fine motor skills

Movers, shakers and players

Aspect:
A Healthy Child

Components:
Growing and developing

Clap Hands! -
feathers and streamers

What you need

* feathers (available from craft or needlework shops)
* ribbons
* chiffon scarves

What you do

1. Blow the feathers into the air for the children to touch. Start by touching them with isolated index fingers and then try clapping to catch the feathers. Sing 'Everybody do this, do this, just like me'.
2. Drop the chiffon scarves from high up and see if the children can clap hands to catch them. Blow them into the air and clap to catch them as they fall.
3. Next, tie ribbons into bundles that will slip gently over the children's wrists. Clap hands together to favourite nursery rhymes, such as 'Baa, Baa, Black Sheep', or 'Jack and Jill'.

another idea:
* Blow bubbles. Pop by clapping hands together.

Ready for more?

* Sing 'Wind the bobbin up' and 'Roly, Poly, Poly', (both in 'This Little Puffin') and practise rolling arms action.
* Take time when washing hands to clap and slide soapy hands together.

Individual needs

☼ Make sure children are sitting straight and if on a chair, have their feet firmly on the ground.

☼ Help children who clap to show their excitement, to use a new word or gesture to make a specific request, eg if they clap excitedly when they see the juice, smile, point to the cup and say, 'Drink'.

Tiny Tip

✴ Don't push children to join in with action rhymes and clapping games. Make it fun. They will join in when they are ready.

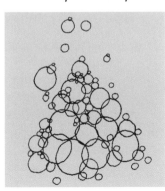

Watch, listen, reflect

👁 Look at the range of different gestures and actions the children are using.

👁 Listen, copy and praise any sounds they make.

👁 Observe what interests each child and helps to hold their attention on an activity or song.

Working together

Parents could:

* share a nursery song and rhyme book with their child.
* make a nursery song part of bedtime routine.

Practitioners could:

* lend nursery rhyme tapes and books to parents.
* give parents the words and movements to their child's favourite action rhymes.

Grab - and let go

Developing fine motor skills

What are they learning?

are they
    using two hands?
    copying actions?
    looking?
    listening?
    making sounds?
    co-ordinating
    hands and eyes?
this leads to
    * fine motor skills
    * mark making

Movers, shakers and players

Aspect:
A Healthy Child

Components:
Growing and developing

Thank You -
offering objects in tower play

What you need
* stacking bricks
* small basket

What you do

1. Build a tower of the bricks and invite the child to come and play. Watch them knock it down! Try to help them wait with a 'Ready, steady', then pause 'Go'.
2. Place all the bricks in the basket. Give them the basket and ask them to pass you a brick. Stretch out your hand. Start to build a tower. Ask the child to pass each brick into your outstretched hand. If they want to help build the tower, take it in turns to pass each other a brick. When the tower is complete, do 'Ready, steady, go' again, encouraging the child to wait for 'Go'.
3. Gather all the bricks together and play again.

another idea:
* Try stacking shoeboxes, or create a very wobbly tower with a selection of junk modelling boxes.

Ready for more?

* Play tea parties, asking the child to offer tiny bits of fruit or bread to other children.
* Play together in the home corner, asking the child to bring you different objects, such as a doll.

Individual needs

☼ Make passing objects into an outstretched hand an important and practical step towards independence of children.

☼ For children needing more help to understand the outstretched hand gesture, ask another adult to gently help the child reach out towards your hand.

Tiny Tip

❋ A gentle tickle on the back of the hand will help reluctant fingers to open!

Watch, listen, reflect

👁 Observe the different natural gestures that each child uses. Think about how much they rely on these gestures and which expressions and phrases they understand without these gesture clues.

👁 Look at the child's body language – are they enjoying sharing and receiving praise?

👁 Listen & note the words they use.

Working together

Parents could:

* encourage their child to pass them items of clothing as they help them to get dressed.
* ask children to choose and pass their bedtime storybook.

Practitioners could:

* think of practical ways to encourage each child's independence.
* practise passing teddy round a small circle of three or four children.

Grab - and let go

Developing fine motor skills

What are they learning?

are they
  anticipating?
  sharing?
  turn taking?
  releasing
  objects?
  reaching out?
this leads to
  * co-operative play
  * communication

Movers, shakers and players

Aspect:
A Healthy Child

Components:
Growing and developing

Fingers and Thumbs -
stickers and stars

What you need

* pens
* small sticky labels
* star stickers

What you do

1. Put a star sticker on each child's and your own index fingers.
2. Sing 'Twinkle Twinkle Little Star' together, pointing index fingers to the sky.
3. Place a star sticker on every finger and thumb, and sing the rhyme again.
4. Help the children to draw a small circle on two plain sticky labels, and add legs to make a spider. Place the spider stickers on the pads of the thumbs. Sing 'Incy, Wincy Spider' with the actions, bringing fingers and thumbs together as the spider climbs the spout.

another idea:

* Draw bird shapes on two stickers and sing the 'Two Little Dickey Birds' rhyme.

Ready for more?

☜ Collect some old bracelets and necklaces and play at putting these on each other and soft toys.
☜ Provide a bowl of cooked noodles for some fun finger play.

Individual needs

☼ Use reflective or fluorescent colours for the stickers for children with visual difficulties.

☼ Place a smiley face sticker on the palm of your hand to encourage reluctant children to get involved with this activity.

☼ Keep the activity very short and focused.

Tiny Tip

❊ Bubbles are brilliant for helping children to isolate their index finger and reach accurately.

Watch, listen, reflect

👁 Observe what motivates the children. What can you do to help them maintain their attention on the activity?

👁 Note the range of gestures used and if children are able to imitate the actions in the rhymes.

👁 Listen for single and two word phrases. Decide if the words used are all object words.

Working together

Parents could:

* try out the star stickers and twinkle twinkle game at home.
* put together a treasure basket of small, but safe objects for their child to explore at home.

Practitioners could:

* enlist the help of parents and volunteers in making finger puppets.
* collect suitable objects for a fingers and thumbs treasure basket.

Grab - and let go

Developing fine motor skills

What are they learning?

are they
   playing together?
   imitating?
   using fingers & thumbs?
   using new words?
this leads to
   * shared attention
   * pencil grip

Movers, shakers and players

Aspect:
A Healthy Child

Components:
Growing and developing

In my Hand -
using brushes and sponges

What you need

* lots of different brushes and sponges (washing up brush or sponge, nail brush, tooth brush, paint brush, cotton buds)
* paint, paint tray, big paper

What you do

1. Tape the paper to the floor. Mix the paint and place in shallow trays with the brushes.
2. Allow plenty of time and freedom for the children to try out the different brushes and experiment with how they can hold and use the brushes.
3. Play alongside the children. Observe the way they are holding the different brushes. Look out for circular movements and also for large up and down paint strokes.
4. Use simple short phrases to describe what they are doing such as 'Pat, pat, pat' or 'Up and down'.

another idea:

* Use large decorators' paintbrushes and a bowl of soapy water outside for painting on the ground and walls.

Ready for more?

* Try painting with big brushes on large cardboard boxes outside. Paint rollers work well and need a different sort of grip and action.
* Dip lengths of ribbon and string in water and make trails outside.

30

Individual needs

☼ Play alongside children who need encouragement. Allow plenty of time for them to watch and perhaps share painting with you.

☼ Give their own paper and paints to children who prefer to work in their own space.

Tiny Tip

✳ Some children will instinctively take a toothbrush to their mouth! Take care, it could be loaded with paint!!

Watch, listen, reflect

👁 Watch how the children grip the brushes and sponges. Look for whole hand palmar grips and finger and thumb pincer grips.

👁 Look at the shapes and movements they are making.

👁 Think about the different ways they are experimenting and finding out about using tools.

Working together

Parents could:

★ let children paint with water in the garden.

★ try wet chalks at home.

Practitioners could:

★ make painting and mark making a part of everyday experiences inside and out.

★ make a list for parents of the sorts of resources they want them to collect, such as decorators' brushes, craft tools and so on.

Grab – and let go

Developing fine motor skills

What are they learning?

are they
    exploring?
    holding?
    using wrist and
    hand?
    watching?
    responding?
this leads to
    * hand control
    * use of tools

**Walkers, talkers
and pretenders**

Aspect:
A Healthy Child
Components:
Growing and
developing

So Small -
tiny bits and pieces
What you need

* doll's tea cups, plates and teaspoons
* dried pasta shapes
* cotton reels
* ribbon, wool and string
* lolly sticks

What you do

1. Give each child a cup and spoon. Sing 'Polly Put the Kettle on' and pretend to stir the tea.
2. Play together, arranging the pasta, string and ribbon bits and cotton reels on the plates as pretend food. Encourage the children to handle each item individually using a precise pincer grip (thumb and first finger together).
3. Invite the children to offer each other items from the plates. Talk about what the food might be, their favourite foods and so on. Encourage and use two word phrases, such as 'Teddy's cup', 'More pasta', 'Look hot!'.

another idea:
* Try this activity in the water tray.

Ready for more?

* Try tracing fingers through or picking up 'hundreds and thousands'.
* Make tiny sandwiches for snack time.
* Give each child a few raisins in a small pot as a treat.

32

Individual needs

☼ Some children will find this activity really hard. Allow plenty of practice, watch carefully and avoid frustration by not making the activity too difficult.

☼ Use special interests such as trains. If a child really likes trains, help them to fix tiny stickers to each coach. Make their interest work for you.

Tiny Tip

❋ Make sure chairs and tables are the right height for children to sit well with their feet on the ground.

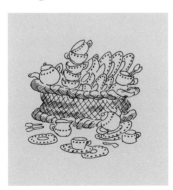

Watch, listen, reflect

👁 Look out for emerging hand preference.

👁 Allow children to use either hand and still encourage children to use two hands together.

👁 Observe turn taking and sharing.

👁 Listen to the way words are used to comment or make requests.

Working together

Parents could:

* give children tiny sweets or raisins one at a time to pick up from their plate.
* play bubbles at home, practise popping and holding the bubble wand.

Practitioners could:

* make sure children are as independent as possible, hanging up their own coats, helping with dressing.
* check there are plenty of finger rhyme books and action rhyme posters for children, parents and staff to share.

Grab - and let go

Developing fine motor skills

What are they learning?

are they
 sharing?
  offering objects?
  handling objects?
  imitating?
this leads to
 * simple pretend play
 * fine motor
 * co-operating

33

Grab - and let go

Developing fine motor skills

Walkers, talkers and pretenders

Aspect:
A Healthy Child

Components:
Growing and developing

34

Gone! - tube play

What you need

* large cardboard tube (ask parents or try a local art or carpet store)
* small cars, buses and trucks

What you do

1. Spread the cars out on the floor and encourage the children to take turns posting the cars down the tube.
2. For each car, do 'Ready, steady, go', with the child waiting for 'Go' before releasing the car into the tube. When it has gone, say and gesture 'Gone'.
3. Ask each child to post a particular car down the tube, perhaps the red car, or the yellow bus and so on.
4. Can the children hold a car in each hand and post them together, or one after the other, down the tube?

another idea:
* Try the same with small balls.

Ready for more?

- Draw pictures on small bits of paper and send them down the tube.
- Post everyday objects into the tube, such as cups, keys, spoons.
- Post buttons down small sweet tubes.

Individual needs

☼ For children with motor difficulties use tennis balls and a larger tube. Make sure the child is well supported and secure.

☼ Use noisy toys such as bells and rattles for children with visual difficulties.

☼ Place a tin lid at the bottom of the tube for extra clang!

Tiny Tip

✳ Shuttlecock and tennis ball containers make great tubes for this play.

Watch, listen, reflect

👁 Watch how the children grasp and manipulate the objects.

👁 See which part of the activity is most rewarding for each child.

👁 Listen and watch how children negotiate turns and interact with each other.

Working together

Parents could:

* try some tube play at home.
* ask around for suitable tubes for you to use in your setting.
* play 'Ready, steady, go' game at home.

Practitioners could:

* decorate the tubes to match a theme or to make them appealing to children.
* use fluorescent paper for children with visual impairment, or perhaps stickers and pictures reflecting a child's special interest.

Grab - and let go

Developing fine motor skills

What are they learning?

are they
    releasing objects?
    listening?
    turn taking?
    sharing?
    using words & gestures?
this leads to
    * sharing fun
    * co-operating
    * attending

Grab - and let go

Developing fine motor skills

Walkers, talkers and pretenders

Aspect:
A Healthy Child
Components:
Growing and developing

Roll it -
rolling and stopping

What you need

* a small ball
* a beach ball
* a big car
* a small car

What you do

1. Sit opposite the children and take it in turns to roll the beach ball between you. Encourage them to roll the ball along the floor and use two hands to stop the ball.
2. Next offer them a choice of the big or small ball. Encourage them to use a combination of words and gestures, or a short phrase. Roll the balls back and forth varying the speed.
3. Play again, giving the children a choice of the big car, or the small car. This time roll the cars to the side of the children so they have to reach to stop the rolling car.

another idea:

* Play at rolling the balls down a plank or slide. Can they stop the beach ball at the bottom of the slide?

Ready for more?

* Roll balls into large cardboard boxes.
* Try rolling cars to land in a garage chalked or taped onto the floor.
* Roll and spin hoops and quoits.

Individual needs

- ☼ Try noisy or scented balls for children with sensory difficulties.
- ☼ Soft squidgey balls are easier for children with motor difficulties.
- ☼ Play lots of passing games with children who have difficulty with the turn taking part of this activity.

Watch, listen, reflect

- Watch how children track the balls and cars.
- Observe how the children take turns and negotiate.
- Listen for short learned phrases, such as 'Ready, steady, go', or 'Here it comes', and so on.

Tiny Tip

❊ Junk box model tubes are great for rolling games.

Working together

Parents could:

* practise rolling and stopping games at home.
* give children lots of opportunity for active outdoor play.

Practitioners could:

* make sure balls, hoops and quoits are easily to hand for rolling games.
* make rolling a fun part of every day routines, such as tidying away.

Grab - and let go

Developing fine motor skills

What are they learning?

are they
- rolling?
- stopping moving objects?
- turn taking?
- enjoying active play?

this leads to
* moving
* hand/eye/body co-ordination

Grab - and let go

Developing fine motor skills

Walkers, talkers and pretenders

Aspect:
A Healthy Child

Components:
Growing and developing

Throw it! - target games

What you need

* beanbags, pairs of socks, soft balls
* chalk
* hoop

What you do

1. Take it in turns to throw the beanbags high in the air. Try throwing the beanbags underarm and then overarm.
2. Make a target with the chalk on the floor. See if you can get the beanbags in the target area. Next, mark the target on the wall and take aim.
3. Roll the socks up in pairs and try throwing them to each other.
4. Play again with the soft balls.
5. Hang the hoop up in the air so that you can practise throwing the socks, balls and beanbags through the hoop.

another idea:

* Try throwing wet sponges at a target outside.

Ready for more?

Pat balloons. See how long you can keep them in the air. Can you pat them through the hoop?

Make a red target for red beanbags and a blue target for blue beanbags.

Individual needs

✿ Use children's special interests to help focus their attention.

✿ Place the target at a distance and height suitable for children with motor difficulties.

✿ Only half inflate the beach ball for easier catching and throwing.

Tiny Tip

✽ Fix footprints to the floor where you want children to stand for throwing and target games.

Watch, listen, reflect

👁 Look how the children grip the ball. Are they focusing on the target?

👁 Listen to the language used to negotiate turns.

👁 Check that the target is positioned to challenge children, but also to give them some chance of success.

Working together

Parents could:

* make throwing a fun part of everyday routines, such as taking turns with their child to throw socks into the drawer, or washing into the machine.

Practitioners could:

* make sure there is a good range of different objects for throwing and target games such as quoits, beanbags, Frisbees, boomerangs and so on.

* plan throwing games for indoor play as well as outside.

Grab - and let go

Developing fine motor skills

What are they learning?

are they
  throwing?
  taking turns?
  making choices?
  having fun with active play?
this leads to
  * co-operative play
  * ball skills
  * confidence

39

Grab - and let go

Developing fine motor skills

Walkers, talkers and pretenders

Aspect:
A Healthy Child

Components:
Growing and developing

Up and Down - making marks

What you need

* large paint brushes
* chalks and paint
* large sheets of paper
* tape (masking tape is easy to use)

What you do

1. Tape the paper to the floor. Play alongside the children making huge up and down whole arm movements. Sing, 'Here we go up, up, up and down', using the tune of 'Here We go Round the Mulberry Bush'.
2. Encourage the children to make big continuous movements. How far can they go before the paint runs out?
3. Try to make circular movements. Can you cover the paper in circles? As they paint or chalk each circle, say 'Round and stop'. Play alongside the children so they can watch and imitate your words and actions.

another idea:
* See if together you can paint a pattern of stripes.

Ready for more?

🖐 Let the children choose different sizes and shapes of paper, eg long thin strips, circles or small rectangles.

🖐 Use wet chalks, letting the children try out the different ways of using the chalks.

40

Individual needs

☼ Make sure that children who dislike getting paint on their hands, have the opportunity to wipe the brush handles clean.

☼ Try fluorescent paint and contrasting paper for children with visual difficulties.

Tiny Tip

✲ Post-it notes and blank sticky labels are a great addition to the mark making area.

Watch, listen, reflect

👁 Look at how the children are holding the brushes and chalks.

👁 Check their grip and encourage them to use their other hand to hold the paper steady.

👁 Listen to their words and phrases. Are they using object words, action words, and describing words?

👁 Observe how the children are relating to each other as they play.

Working together

Parents could:

* make sure that their child can get pens and paper, without asking.
* help their child to make marks on birthday cards, shopping lists and so on.
* sit with their child as they write, fill in forms, sign cards, write letters.

Practitioners could:

* talk with parents about the importance of mark making.
* check the mark making area is well equipped, clean, tidy and appealing to the children.

What are they learning?

are they
imitating lines?
scribbling circles?
playing alongside?
attending?
this leads to
* mark making
* pencil grip
* listening
* attending

Grab - and let go

Developing fine motor skills

Walkers, talkers and pretenders

Aspect:
A Healthy Child

Components:
Growing and developing

42

Paint Magic -
drips and drops

What you need
* plastic droppers and syringes
* fine paint brushes
* thin straws
* strips of paper
* paint

What you do
1. Add water to the paint to make a runny consistency. Spread out the strips of paper.
2. Dip the brushes and straws into the paint and very carefully let the paint drip from the brush onto the paper. Can you make trails and squiggles?
3. Use the droppers and plastic syringes to drop tiny amounts of paint onto the paper.
4. Help the children to work carefully, using fingers and thumbs to hold the paint tools and to watch closely so that the paint falls onto the paper strips.

another idea:
* Try this on different types of paper, such as blotting paper or corrugated card.

Ready for more?
🖐 Draw a line from left to right across the strips of paper. See if the children can drip paint from left to right along the line.
🖐 Make drippy pictures outside with soapy water onto the ground.

Individual needs

☼ Try using washing up sponges with handles in drippy paint for children with fine motor difficulties.

☼ Wrap tape around paintbrushes to make chunkier handles for easier grip.

☼ Dab rather than drip paint for children at an earlier developmental level.

Tiny Tip

�֎ Add a plastic funnel and clear tubing to water play with small squeezy bottles and droppers.

Watch, listen, reflect

👁 Watch for emerging hand preferences.

👁 Look to see if children are using their other hand to hold the paper steady.

👁 Listen for describing words, such as those for colour and consistency - thick, thin, drip, drop, runny.

Working together

Parents could:

* try plastic droppers, syringes and squeezy bottles at bath time.

* run their finger along the print from left to right when reading to their child.

Practitioners could:

* use MDF and chalk board paint to make a chalk board for outside. Fix your chalk board securely to a wall.

* check out DIY, kitchen-ware and craft stores for squeezy bottles, droppers and plastic syringes.

Grab - and let go

Developing fine motor skills

What are they learning?

are they
  controlling fingers and hands?
  describing?
  working from left to right?
  exploring?
this leads to
  * tripod grip
  * mark making
  * creativity

Grab - and let go

Developing fine motor skills

Aspect:
A Healthy Child

Components:
Growing and developing

Resources

Things to collect

Contrasting black & white toys & pictures
Different textured fabrics
Baby safety mirrors
Stickers
Hats, bracelets and bangles
Brushes and scrunchies
Bells, rattles
Ribbons
Flannels and sponges
Cardboard tubes
Balls of every size and texture
Hoops, rings and quoits

Brushes and rollers
Buy:
* decorators' brushes and rollers from DIY stores
* pastry brushes and pastry cutting rollers from cookshops
* baby hairbrushes from baby shops
* nail brushes and tooth brushes
* dishwashing and cleaning brushes from bargain shops
* craft rollers from art shops

Cardboard tubes
Try:
* carpet shops
* fabric shops
* packing and office suppliers
* printers

Very small items
Try:
* hundreds and thousands and sugar strands from the cake making bit of the supermarket
* pasta stars and shapes

Songs and rhymes

These songs and rhymes are all suitable for developing hands, fingers, feet and fine motor skills.

Finger rhymes and nursery songbooks

'The Little Book of Nursery Rhymes' (Featherstone Education)
'Carousel Nursery Rhymes CD' (available from Featherstone Education)
'This Little Puffin' (Penguin Books)
'The Collins Book of Nursery Rhymes' (Collins)
'Bobby Shaftoe' (A&C Black)
'Lucy Collins Big Book of Nursery Rhymes' (Macmillan)
'Okki Tokki Unga - Action Songs for Children' (A&C Black)

Finger Rhymes to aid fine motor control

This Little Pig Went to Market
Pat-a-Cake, Pat-a-Cake
Round and Round the Garden
She Didn't Dance
Incy Wincy Spider
Tommy Thumb
Five Little Peas
Two Little Dicky Birds
Wind the Bobbin

My Little House
Here are the Lady's Knives & Forks
Here is a Box
One Potato, Two Potato
Peter Hammers with One Hammer
One Finger, One Thumb Keep Moving
Heads, Shoulders, Knees and Toes
Roly, Poly Up and Down
Teddy Bear, Teddy Bear

Aspect:
A Healthy Child
Components:
Growing and
developing

The Little Baby Book Series

The structure of Little Baby Books has been developed to support the Birth to Three Matters Guidance, issued by the Department for Education and Science and the Sure Start Unit in 2003. Each series has been structured to follow closely the aspects contained within the guidance, and to provide practitioners with practical help implementing and following the guidance. Little Baby Books are particularly useful for planning.

The Little Baby Books series contains 16 books in 4 sets of 4, all available from Featherstone Education.

Purple Books support the development of a Strong Child:
a child who is secure, confident and aware of him/herself, feeling a valued and important member of their family, their group and their setting.

Pink Books support the development of a Skilful Communicator:
a child who is sociable, good at communicating with adults and other children, listens and communicates with confidence, who enjoys and plays with words in discussion, stories, songs and rhymes.

Green Books support the development of a Competent Learner:
a child who uses play to explore and make sense of their world, creating, imagining, and representing their experiences.

Blue Books support the development of a Healthy Child:
a child who is well nourished and well supported, feels safe and protected, and uses that sense of security to grow, both physically and emotionally, becoming independent and able to make choices in their play and learning.

	A Strong Child	A Skilful Communicator	A Competent Learner	A Healthy Child
Series 1	I Like You, You Like Me (me, myself & I; a sense of belonging)	What I Really Want (being together; finding a voice)	Touch It, Feel It (being imaginative; being creative)	Grab & Let Go (growing & developing)
Series 2	Look At Me (me, myself & I; being acknowledged & affirmed)	What's That? (finding a voice)	Count With Me (making connections)	Tickle & Tumble (keeping safe)
Series 3	I Can Do It (developing self assurance)	Let's Listen (listening & responding)	Make Your Mark (representing)	Which One? (making healthy choices)
Series 4	Me & My World (a sense of belonging)	Get The Message (making meaning)	Let's Explore (being creative)	Me & You (emotional wellbeing)

All the above are available direct from the publisher, or from your usual book supplier.
Please phone for details.

©Featherstone Education Ltd, 2003
Text © Sally Featherstone, Clare Beswick, 2003
Illustrations © Martha Hardy, 2003
Series Editor, Sally Featherstone

First published in the UK, 2003

The right of Sally Featherstone and Clare Beswick to be identified as authors of this work has been asserted in accordance with Sections 77 and 78 of the Copyright, Designs and Patents Act, 1988.

All rights reserved. No part of this publication may be reproduced by any means, stored in a retrieval system, or transmitted in any form or by any means, electronic, mechanical, photocopying, recording or otherwise, without the prior written consent of the publisher. This book may not be lent, sold, hired out or otherwise disposed of by way of trade in any form of binding or with any cover other than that in which it is published without the prior consent of the publisher, and without this condition being imposed upon the subsequent user.

Published in the United Kingdom by
Featherstone Education Ltd
44 - 46 High Street
Husbands Bosworth
Leicestershire
LE17 6LP